Healing through Writing

Hope this helps you on your journey, baby ♡

— Ashikha & Shirish

Healing through Writing

◆

A Journaling Guide to Emotional and Spiritual Growth

Anthony D. Parnell, M.S.W.

iUniverse, Inc.
New York Lincoln Shanghai

Healing through Writing
A Journaling Guide to Emotional and Spiritual Growth

Copyright © 2005, 2007 by Anthony Dwane Parnell

All rights reserved. No part of this book may be used or reproduced by any means, graphic, electronic, or mechanical, including photocopying, recording, taping or by any information storage retrieval system without the written permission of the publisher except in the case of brief quotations embodied in critical articles and reviews.

iUniverse books may be ordered through booksellers or by contacting:

iUniverse
2021 Pine Lake Road, Suite 100
Lincoln, NE 68512
www.iuniverse.com
1-800-Authors (1-800-288-4677)

The views expressed in this work are solely those of the author and do not necessarily reflect the views of the publisher, and the publisher hereby disclaims any responsibility for them.

ISBN-13: 978-0-595-34642-4 (pbk)
ISBN-13: 978-0-595-79387-7 (ebk)
ISBN-10: 0-595-34642-1 (pbk)
ISBN-10: 0-595-79387-8 (ebk)

Printed in the United States of America

Contents

Introduction xi

Part I The Journal as a Personal Collage

The Journal 3
- *Poetry* 5
- *Daily Narratives* 13
- *Letters to Self* 16
- *Dreams* 18
- *Synchronistic Events* 20
- *Significant Events* 22
- *Random Thoughts/Daily Life Questions* 24
- *Goals* 27

Opening Up 36
- *The Power of Beliefs* 36
- *Rebuilding Your System of Beliefs* 44
- *Picking Up the Pen* 47
  - DAY 1 50
  - DAY 2 51
  - DAY 3 52
  - DAY 4 53
  - DAY 5 54

Part II Emotional and Spiritual Growth

Growth and Inner Healing 61

Stages of Emotional and Spiritual Growth.................... 64
Seven Determinants of Emotional and Spiritual Growth........... 67
Shaping Our Daily Reality................................. 75

Appendix A Beliefs Exercises 77
Appendix B Definitions of Love and Happiness 79
Appendix C Anger Management Plan 81
Appendix D Stress Management Plan..................... 83
References 87
Empowerment Workshops 89

Acknowledgements

I would like to express my sincere appreciation to all of the individuals who have supported my efforts to complete this book and, in general, have supported my aspirations as a writer, artist and entrepreneur. I also would like to thank the many "self-help" authors who have had the courage to share their life experiences and knowledge about healing and the growth process. Your words of wisdom and encouragement gave me hope in many of the same ways, in times of despair and self-doubt, that I hope this book will do for others.

FREEDOM

For so longggg,
I tried to break free
Of this feeling
Of internal pain.

I was a wounded soul
In the midst of others
But still feeling
Alone and ashamed.

A gift of words
Became my escape
My only hope
For breaking free.

I summoned Courage
Inner Strength & Wisdom
Until I could taste my Spiritual Victory.

Still, many years went by
Before I discovered
Who and what I was born and meant to be.

Shattering my notions of Love,
Of worldly ambitions, and
The essence of everything
I once believed.

Redefining the ultimate goal
That I would wholeheartedly choose
To pursue
in this Lifetime.

Now
Believing that a Life of wholeness,
Balance & Love
Would be the greatest joy
I could ever find.

Introduction

Healing through Writing is a workbook designed to assist individuals in facilitating their emotional and spiritual growth. Also, it is a philosophy in which emphasis is placed on expanding self-awareness and a sense of personal responsibility for the shape and direction of one's life. For, in light of the growing emphasis in our culture on individuals seeking emotional support and guidance from a professional therapist, the question I've asked myself a thousand times is, "What did we do before therapy existed?" In essence, this question relates directly to the rapidly changing concepts and beliefs about family and religion being viewed and utilized as the primary vehicle for emotional support and guidance. Even greater is the question, "What does formalized, professional therapy have to offer individuals that family and religion can not?" Maybe the answer is as simple as, "It depends on the person and the circumstances." While I am not arguing against individuals seeking formalized therapy, I am strongly opposed to individuals being encouraged or led to believe that there is greater wisdom to be found in a therapist's office than in their individual faith and the physical and emotional support of loving family and friends. Fundamentally, then, my argument is that individuals possess greater personal power and wisdom than is often realized or exercised.

Healing through Writing utilizes various writing methods to illustrate the benefits of writing in a journal on a daily or consistent basis. Developed as a direct result of my personal experiences confronting many of the daily challenges of life, *Healing through Writing* incorporates techniques that I have found useful in managing stress and in facilitating a process of emotional and spiritual growth in my personal life. Techniques and philosophies discussed in this book also derive from knowledge gained in my ten years of professional experience as a mental health therapist and social worker. In my profession, I have worked closely with individuals experiencing difficulty coping with various life circumstances and emotional challenges. As a therapist, my task is to help individuals who are in crisis or experience high levels of stress or anxiety to identify strengths and resources. Unfortunately, in many instances, the full range of needed resources is not immediately available. These individuals, therefore, are further challenged to utilize internal resources such as faith, determination, perseverance, and positive thinking to resolve or cope more effectively with their current life dilemma. While resources may be immediately available to some people, there may be other barriers to establishing a trusting therapeutic relationship. Some of us may express resistance to receiving help in a formal therapeutic setting simply because of the stigma of participating in therapy. Additionally, there may be resistance between the therapist and client due to differences of gender, age, or race.

Given my experiences with resistant and more challenging clients, I intensely began to ask myself, "What can be done to provide help to individuals who are motivated to receive help but have difficulty receiving it in the context of a formal client-therapist relationship?" Should I give them 300 page books to read? Should I step out of the boundaries of my professional role and agree to be their friend? The only answer I could find was to offer them what had been working for me for more than 6 years. It was writing any and everything I felt and thought in a journal, constantly reexamining it as part of a process of finding solutions to my emotional dilemmas and daily life questions.

I started writing at the age of 22, when I first began journaling on a daily basis. I would just spontaneously write poems at any time of the day or night, in public or private, and eventually began to write about daily events and my reactions to them. At the age of 25, I self-published a collection of poems entitled, *In Search of Soul* where I described my journey to find love in a soul mate and within my soul. At the age of 27, I self-published a second collection of poems entitled *Mind Games,* which encouraged the readers to become more aware of the ways in which they might be more of an obstacle to their happiness and peace, rather than other individuals and the environment in which they lived. By then, my writing had obviously taken me to a much deeper place of spiritual and emotional awareness. Though writing my way through my emotional challenges never excluded the necessity to feel love and support from others, it was a critical piece to my accepting full responsibility for my emotional and spiritual challenges.

In 1998, at the age of 29, I decided to write my autobiography, and this highlighted a process of self-discovery. I did not have the intent of publishing it. It was simply the result of many life events and their impact coming to the surface of my consciousness. For several years, I had been practicing letting go in writing as I was compelled and inspired by the creative flow of the moment. However, the process of writing my autobiography was a daily process that continued for two consecutive months. In going with this flow, I relived many of the traumatic experiences of my childhood and other painful experiences of my adulthood. While the process was very therapeutic, it also revealed that even though I had already for a number of years spent a lot of time and energy committed to healing old wounds, there still was a need for much more healing.

This was very surprising, given that a year earlier, after publishing *Mind Games,* I thought that I had finally uncovered all of the debris of my emotional scars. For, I had been inspired to publish *Mind Games* after having, for a brief period of time, existed on the brink of suicide. I had grown weary of waiting to feel a sense of peace and happiness in my life. I was tired of questioning the meaning of life or why less compassionate individuals seemed to prosper while the compassionate ones seemed poor and powerless. Having made countless journal entries and written thousands of poems reflecting the impact of being abandoned by my father at the age of 12 and of my mother's suicide when I was 14, I thought that by then I should have completed the process of healing old wounds. Nonetheless, healing proved to be a long term process that I had greatly underestimated. Subsequently, the enduring of many lonely hours of silence and the tears peeling off the layers and layers of hurt and pain that had taken a toll on my mind and body ultimately left me drained of energy and hope.

I desperately wanted to believe that I was not placed on this earth to suffer and that my life had purpose and meaning. I felt like lashing out on others, which I often did. But, still not achieving my desired results, I began to internalize my feelings of anger and frustration. It wasn't until I admitted to myself that I was the only person who had the ability to change how I felt about myself and accepted full responsibility for the outcome of my life that the words I wrote in my journal began to have a transforming quality on my life and on circumstances that were enduring. This was coupled with the realization at the brink of suicide that I did not want to die. I just didn't want to feel like a victim of circumstances that were beyond my control. In essence, I was internally challenged to look in the mirror of my life and be completely honest with myself. The truth I uncovered was that I didn't fully believe in myself. Yet, as a grown man, I could no longer choose to blame my current emotional and psychological limitations on what happened in my childhood.

In this moment of revelation, I also realized that I still had not given myself permission to fully feel and express all of what I felt, thought and believed. In self-publishing two books of poetry, I had made tremendous progress and discovered an avenue for healthy self-expression, but I still had been unable to move from anger and pain to love and happiness because I still felt a deep sense of guilt about many circumstances in my life. Moreover, I had become frustrated with the process of emotional and spiritual growth because I didn't fully grasp the long-term commitment that was required to not only attain but also to maintain wholeness and balance in my life.

It took some time, but I slowly began to develop a more realistic expectation of my process of emotional and spiritual growth. I realized and began to accept that wholeness and balance are not fixed states of being. Rather, they are states of existence that constantly must be nurtured and maintained by exercising daily awareness. With this new insight, I was prepared to recommit myself to continuing to be honest with myself about what I think, feel, and believe in each and every moment of my existence, regardless of the daily challenges I face. This recommitment to continuous honesty and authenticity in my daily life led me to understand what was essential for preventing the buildup of negative energy, further fueling my emotional and spiritual growth.

I discovered enough faith in life and within myself to keep moving forward in life. Subsequently, I increasingly moved to a place of greater acceptance with who I am as a person and with the limitations I felt existed in many of my relationships with others and the world in which I live. This self-evolution and expansion of self-awareness also entailed my gaining tremendous clarity about why I had chosen to pursue a career in social work. It was now evident that my decision to obtain a master's of social work degree was not only for the purpose of helping others. I was unconsciously seeking to find a way to help myself. I was desperately searching for answers to my own problems and internal struggles that other individuals had not been able to fully provide. I felt an intense desire to help others because I intimately knew the feeling of no one being able to say or to put into words what I was going through. I had felt the anger and disappointment of friends and family wanting to help but not being able to do so. This was because they could not relate to some of my life experiences or had not yet found a way to overcome their own emotional wounding.

Healing through Writing, consequently, represents the culmination of my efforts to incorporate my knowledge as a social worker and therapist with my positive experiences confronting life challenges. It utilizes writing as a method for managing stress and facilitates personal growth. Reading books focused on these issues have been of great benefit in the 13 years that I have been committed to journaling on a daily basis. However, I have found journaling to have a tremendous value. Initially, journaling provided me with an outlet solely for voicing my emotions privately when I was not feeling confident or comfortable in sharing my thoughts or emotions with others. Now, journaling encompasses more than just a vehicle for self-expression. It is a means by which I can process my thoughts and emotions irrespective of the support or insight of others. It represents a sounding board through which I can observe and assess patterns of behavior and thought in my life.

Healing through Writing is an illustration of how past experiences can be used to enlighten the present when an individual is willing to focus on how thoughts and beliefs shape our everyday reality more than our environment—the people, places, and things around us. Originally designed for a workshop format, the philosophy and techniques presented have evolved over time as a synthesis of my beliefs about personal development. As it happens, in my earlier experiences participants frequently expressed that in the workshops we barely touched the surface in discussing how various types of information and tools can be used to facilitate growth and inner healing. Thus, my ultimate goal was set to contribute to the growing body of literature available to individuals searching for ways to facilitate their own healing and personal growth by offering a personalized testimony of what has worked for myself, for my clients, and, most importantly, for ordinary people.

PART I
The Journal as a Personal Collage

The Journal

Clearly, most people's idea of a journal is that it is about writing love poems or secrets to be hidden from the world. While journals should be private, the *Healing through Writing* concept of journaling is much broader, viewing personal writing as not only about romance or embarrassing events. It encompasses any and everything within the scope of our daily life experiences, what I like to refer to as "The Collage of Your Life." Thus, the journal serves as a storehouse in which our life experiences can be documented. First and foremost, the journal is not expected to conform to any style, category, or representation and neither should it have any discernible meaning. It only needs to have substance and value for you, the writer.

Ultimately, what one documents in one's journal should become a reference tool to one's own life—its progress, its regress, its challenges, or its milestones. Not only will it allow one to reflect on it, it will also help one to identify one's spiritual and emotional center on a daily basis. It's as though the only focus becomes "the here and now," whereby one is constantly asking oneself, "What is the question of the moment? What am I supposed to be learning? What is life currently trying to teach me (as revealed by one's responses to everyday experiences)?" It is with this focus that one explores and writes one's dominating thoughts and emotions to discover what they are able to reveal about where one is in relation to "The Now of Life."

There are many advantages to keeping a daily journal. One benefit is that journaling, much like exercise, therapy, talking to friends, sex, or many other hobbies or recreational activities, offers an avenue for releasing emotions that have the potential of negatively impacting one's well-being. A secondary benefit is that journaling provides an opportunity for one to increase or develop his or her ability to express his or her thoughts or emotions through writing. For individuals who already possess a broad range of awareness of their emotions or a high level of writing proficiency but have difficulty dealing with the intensity of their emotions, journaling is an excellent tool for reviewing one's behavior and reactions to prior situations. By referring to prior experiences, one is able to gauge the appropriateness of one's reactions to others while learning to develop healthier responses.

Thirdly, journaling is an excellent tool for expanding self-awareness. It is a mirror of the self: of one's perceptions of and responses to life's events. Furthermore, journaling is a means by which one's process of development can be recorded. By documenting events in one's life, the journal can serve as a self-documentary in which one's thoughts and emotions are captured at a particular point in time.

Journaling is also representative of self-dialogue in that it challenges the writer to distinguish subjective from objective responses. In writing on a daily basis, it is possible to increase one's ability to process information and improve the effectiveness of decision-making. When reviewing emotional content in one's journal, one can observe situations and circumstances from a different point of view. To be sure, it could provide a library of self-information that can be accessed in the present to identify healthy coping mechanisms or to later reflect on previous challenges and obstacles and how they were overcome.

The ultimate goal of writing is to find our own center of emotional balance and to identify ways to regain balance when confronted with emotional dilemmas. In committing ourselves to the growth process, we then can begin to develop self-awareness to achieve and maintain emotional and spiritual balance in our lives. Journaling and other forms of creative expression are tools, which can assist us in developing the self-awareness needed to recognize when we are not emotionally or spiritually centered. Equally, they can also assist us in restoring emotional balance when unable to do so without some form of external support.

POETRY

Poetry is one of the most popular and most convenient forms of self-expression. Due to the short amount of time it generally requires one to write a poem, one can immediately begin processing one's thoughts and emotions. This is unlike the time it may take to compose a song or to draw a painting. Poetry is perfect for the immediate expression of one's emotions if one has acquired the ability to find the right words and to put them in the right sequence with rhythm. Poetry is an art form that is similar to music, dance, and drama in which a wide range of emotions from happy to sad, or from excitement to depression can be captured.

Poetry, in addition to releasing emotions that have the potential of negatively influencing one's well being provides a mirror for self-examination. It is a means by which one can observe one's thoughts and feelings from another point of view. I have frequently found that even some of the seemingly simplistic and shorter poems I have written have taken days, weeks, and sometimes months to fully comprehend their meaning. The following pages include examples of how poetry can be used to express a variety of emotions in a variety of forms. Additionally, a number of other original poems are presented throughout this workbook to further illustrate the range of thought and emotion that can be captured through poetry and how this form of writing has assisted me in my personal process of healing.

"The Power of Words"

Words have the Power
    To change
What we think.   How we Feel.

And, the way   In which
    We choose to Live
        Our Lives
Even though
    It may take time
        Before Our Dreams
            Materialize.

Words have the Power
To Change   All Things....

For, it all begins
With the Words
We Speak to Ourselves
In those Silent
      Dark Places
            Where Light Begins
                  To Shine!!!

"More Than Words…"

Poetry,
Is more than
Words.

For,
Self-Expression
Does not begin
with Words.

It begins
With the Courage
To allow ourselves
To Feel.

And Poetry
Is a Form
Of Self-Expression
That Validates
What we Think,
Feel and Believe

Though known by Many,
Poetry is Understood
By Few.

Because Poetry
Is more than Wordssss.

Poetry is a Way
Of Life.

Poetry,
Is the Expression
Of the Reality of Our Lives
From Moment to Moment

That is Why Poetry
Has Become....

The Words of My Life.

RAGE

The time has come
To face yourself
And rejoice
In the birth of a new day.
The time has come
To heal yourself by letting love
Make a way,
Blaze a trail of tears.

The time has come
To face yourself
By seeing the reality
Of your pain,
And not hiding
In shame
But embracing it

Even to the point of rage.

MY EMOTIONAL HOUSE

I write...Because,
It is what I Feel.
It is what I Think.

I write because,
My intellectual world
And
My emotional world
Are in harmony.

I write because,
The things I think
And, the things I feel
You may not fully understand
Or support.

But, no longer does it matter.
Because, it is
My emotional house.

And, this
is where I
choose to live.

THE VALLEY OF OUR FEARS

From Fear to Fear
It seems we move
Trying to overcome

Yet, it grapples us
Deep Inside
Disabling us from Movement
Free as the Wind.

Yes, We want to be Free
Free to allow
Our Inner Soul to Guide.

But, new visions of courage
Are yet to arrive
And, so we continue
To Hide
Behind Guilt, Doubt
And Inner Inhibitions.

Our inability to fully believe
In the fulfillment
Of Our Dreams
Becomes our Mental Condition.

Until one day, when we
Finally arrive at that place
Where we can no longer Hide
From the Fear that consumes us

We experience that sacred moment
When something Spiritual
Moves us
To a Higher Plane.

This is that moment
When we finally believe
That we can achieve the dream
We were meant to claim.

And, because
We did not stop.

We now view
The Valley of Our Fears
From the Mountain Top.

DAILY NARRATIVES

Daily Narratives are statements about current events, thoughts, and recurring themes in one's life. These statements are based upon self-observation and most frequently serve as a mirror of the growing self. Through daily recordings, one captures patterns of thinking and behavior during a particular period of time or possibly during a life transition. Such patterns and cycles, generally, are identified when one begins to experience a high degree of awareness and intensity of introspection. Because of this, Daily Narratives are often biographical in nature, consistently referring to one's relationships with others and focusing on developing one's ability to more effectively deal with others in personal relationships. The writer also, in reviewing previously recorded journal entries, is able to assess progress in his or her efforts to resolve emotional dilemmas and interpersonal conflicts.

Example #1

Then it hit me that part of my difficulty is understanding the excuses that people keep making. I haven't made any excuses. No one genuinely feels a need to apologize or ask for forgiveness. They are content to say they did their best. Better yet, they have no desire to change. They see no need to change. The only motivation they have to try and appear as though they're changing is that they're growing old and they fear being alone. That's why they're knocking at my door.

My childhood and early adulthood were a living hell. A living nightmare. Never enough love. Sometimes no love. Never enough food. Sometimes no food. Always afraid to ask for anything—had to think of a speech before asking. Then you were interrogated and yelled at—Mental Torture.

I stopped asking people to be perfect a long time ago. But if they can't be real and express love, "Why do I need them in my life?" I guess I'm coming to the conclusion that I don't. I'm already alone. I've cut people off before, but it was with bitterness, anger, and frustration. And I had absolutely nothing to say to them. Now, it's just that I'm realizing that dealing with people who are basically the same reminds me too much of how things used to be.

10/23/96

Example # 2

Today, I felt tired all day. It's been a very long week. I've been on a plane to and from Akron, Ohio, for a funeral, returned to work and haven't slept for more than five consecutive hours in the last week. On top of that, I'm still grieving the passing of my maternal grandfather. It's such a strange feeling to feel so much sadness given the tension and the conflicts that constantly existed between us throughout our relationship.

Yet, in my maturity as a man, I've learned to value and appreciate the many lessons taught by my grandfather rather than focus on things that I disliked about him. For once, I learned to see and understand the deep love that he had for me, my brother, and sister. This was evident in the sacrifice he made to raise us after the passing of our mother. This in and of itself was a powerful act, despite his inadequacies in conveying warmth and nurturance due to his rigid concept of maleness—of what it means to be a man. So, ultimately, I am more than grateful to my grandfather for the things he shared with me in his life and the role he assumed in my life. I grew to experience a bond with him by gaining a greater understanding of his guidance and protection.

1/22/95

Example #3

August 16, 1996

I had a restless night's sleep. I remember waking up at about 3a.m. Difficulty going to work. Felt Anger. Couldn't fully resolve before going to work. When I came home, I went within myself. It was difficult getting to the source. I eventually identified a lot of Aggression...an emotion similar to anger that is not directed at anyone in particular. It's a feeling like I could go off on someone.

After getting fully in touch with this energy, I, for the first time I can recall, focused all of this energy on to something else. I pictured having my own company...being free of people standing over me (At work they decided to give me a pager...This really drives me crazy...Freedom). Rather than focusing on what upsets me, I focused on what I want to materialize.

Does my aggression scare me?

Does the aggression of others scare
Or intimidate me?

Does my aggression scare or intimidate
Other people?

August 17, 1996

I woke up this morning feeling more aggression. I should not be afraid of this. I need to remind myself that the problem is not aggression. The problem is what I do with aggression.

If I suppress it I'm waiting for an explosion to happen. A part of me is afraid that because I'm having these thoughts, I'm going to draw this kind of situation to myself. Better still, I need to remind myself that it is the thoughts that I focus on or ignore that eventually manifest.

LETTERS TO SELF

Letters to Self are also useful in addressing emotional issues in one's relationships with others. Yet, they give one the option of giving a letter to someone else or keeping it for oneself after realizing that it would do more harm than good. In writing letters to oneself, one may realize the need to focus more on one's ability to accept things as they are rather than expect the other person to change. This is the greatest therapeutic value to be found in Letters to Self. When writing with the intent of giving a letter to the individual with whom one has recently had a conflict or with whom one has unresolved issues, one can view conflicts both subjectively and objectively. After writing it, one can imagine how the reader will respond.

The goal in writing Letters to Self is to discover that the greatest benefit in writing them derives from a release of tensions in a non-confrontational manner. This method of writing also gives one an opportunity to process one's emotions and determine the most effective way of addressing the other person and dealing with unresolved issues. One, therefore, has to challenge oneself to confront these issues and deal with them in a healthy manner, even if the other party is either unavailable or resistant to discussing or acknowledging them.

Example #1   (Joe borrowing money)

How can you call yourself a friend? You asked me to lend you $100 and said that you would pay it when you got paid on the 15th of the month. Not only did you not pay it, but after I finally hunted you down, and you gave me a check, I went to the bank and they said your account was closed. You have no idea how frustrating this is and how much this hurts as a friend.

Example #2

Do you have emotional needs that I just don't understand? Well, I shouldn't say that I don't understand. I just have different needs than you. It is particularly frustrating when you are asking me to be more emotionally supportive of you than I need you to be of me. 90% of the time, I am able to work through my emotions on my own, but it doesn't work the other way around, even though you're more mature and independent than most women.

I feel like this is why you and other women chose me as a companion—not just to hang out at the movies and for dinner and dancing. Because I'm a good listener and I can be emotionally responsive, this seems to make you and other women I've dated want it more and more and to expect it at all times. They get to the point where they don't care if I don't have the energy to give it or if my mind is preoccupied with other things. Maybe, my love is conditional or I just am not willing to make the same compromises most other men are willing to make. I need my needs to be met in order to give a woman what she wants in return. Then, and only then, will I feel it's worth it.

DREAMS

Recording dreams in my journal has been one of the most surprising benefits of journaling. For years, I did not have a particular fascination for or interest in dreams or their interpretation primarily because I rarely remembered them. However, in the last few years, as I have increasingly become more in tune with my subconscious thoughts, I have found greater correlation between what was happening in my life and what I was dreaming.

I had heard of people recording their dreams in a dream book, and, as I began to recall mine more frequently, I experimented with ways of recording and interpreting them. Most importantly, I learned to see more consistently the symbolism of many of my dreams and how they portrayed current issues in my daily existence. My focus, then, became to interpret them in light of current challenges and life events, such as the death of a loved one, intimate relationships, career decisions and so on. My goal was to identify the unconscious internal struggles so that I can solve my emotional dilemmas.

Below are a few basic examples of how I recorded themes or ideas that I recalled from my dreams:

Example #1:

"I was with a beautiful girl. She asked us to take something out of her friend's car and put it in the house. When she dropped us off, a gang was coming down the street, so we went the other way. Another gang was coming from the opposite direction, so we crossed the street. We could feel the tension in the air. We headed up an alley and a guy from the neighborhood said, "Don't go to your left." I looked in his eyes and said, "Are you sure" (to decide whether or not we should trust him). He said, "Yeah." As we ran in the opposite direction, my younger brother started crying. I said, "Shut up or I'm leaving you."

Themes: Tired of Responsibility for others; Trust (who can you?). Going with the flow (living in the moment). Feeling Trapped.

Example #2:

I was riding in a car with one of my sisters and one of my brothers, who was driving. We headed to Santa Barbara, a town about two hours outside of L.A., to visit some of my friends (a couple). I wanted them to see my friend's house that overlooked the ocean. My brother wouldn't listen to the directions I was trying to give him and took us about 1 hour off course.

We stopped at a trailer home park and there was a man near the entrance waiting to greet someone, and he thought we were the people he was expecting. He walked towards us and extended his hand to shake our hand. I said, "I'm sorry, but we're not the people you've been waiting for." We got back in the car and took off on the highway again. I woke up from the dream shortly thereafter, but I don't remember ever arriving at the house in Santa Barbara.

Themes: My dreaming about having a house like my friends; visualizing my own wealth and prosperity. Wanting to share my dreams, visions, and future wealth with my family; wanting them to prosper along with me. Allowing someone else to drive when I'm the one who knows where I'm going.

SYNCHRONISTIC EVENTS

Webster defines synchronicity as, "To take place or cause to take place at the same time." In my mind, a synchronistic event is one in which I am alarmed by the timeliness of an event occurring in my life. My belief is that a certain message can be spontaneously given to me when a person appears in my life to assist me in moving in a previously determined direction. Therefore, an intense wish or desire is fulfilled, or I can possibly even be provided with answers to a life question. For instance, the phone may ring at the exact moment that I was thinking of someone or trying to make a major life decision. Or better yet, when dead broke, I have coincidentally opened an old book and found a $20 bill. Recording synchronistic events gives me a sense of being more aware and in tune with my surroundings. In addition, it challenges me to live more fully in the moment given that there often is greater meaning to be found in our interactions or sometimes brief encounters with others.

Examples

Synchronistic Event (March 1994)

I can't believe that I'll be graduating with my Masters of Social Work degree in two months (May 1994). Now, the most difficult part seems to be deciding where I'm going to live and work after I graduate. My first choice is Los Angeles because I love being in warm weather and I would like to be close to my father again. And, visiting New Orleans this weekend confirmed for me that I wouldn't be happy in that town long-term. Jacksonville did seem like the perfect decision given that it's a growing city. But, suddenly receiving this phone call from a U-Haul customer service representative seems more than coincidental. In many ways, it seems like a sign from God trying to help me move to Los Angeles.

Can you believe it? Because of the major earthquake that just happened in L.A., U-Haul is offering a one-way rental special for $600 across country. This includes towing my car. People are dying to get out of L.A. I could be reading more into this assuming it's a spiritual message. Either way, at least I reserved the rate on my credit card, for now, taking it as confirmation that I am making the right decision.

Synchronistic Event (September 26, 2004)

An appraiser was standing on the sidewalk in front of my house as I pulled into the driveway on lunch break from work. His name was Wendell Merritt. I had scanned across his name in the yellow pages two days before, as I desperately sought an appraiser to expedite my efforts to refinance my home. He had a very pleasant demeanor, and I suspected that he was not from Los Angeles. The truth was that he was born and raised in my hometown of Akron, Ohio, and had moved to Los Angeles in 1953. I took a chance and called my oldest maternal uncle in Akron, Ohio who is popular and knows a lot of people in Akron. He happened to be at home having taken the day off of work. While we were in the backyard I handed Mr. Merritt the phone. He and my uncle talked for nearly 20 minutes straight. I couldn't believe that he grew up with my maternal grandfather around the corner from my great grandparents' house.

I was suddenly able to understand the reason for the many delays in my finding an appraiser. I was supposed to meet Mr. Merritt. I had been missing my maternal and paternal grandfather. I had been having recurring dreams about my ancestors as I was realizing that I no longer had a close connection to any elders for wisdom or to feel comfort in their presence. But, in meeting Wendell, I felt reconnected to my ancestors.

SIGNIFICANT EVENTS

Significant Events are events that have special meaning to you for a variety of personal reasons, such as anniversaries, birthday celebrations and so on. The notion of recording significant events in your journal may sound simplistic, but such events can provide excellent references when reflecting on past experiences. In recording these events and the dates of their occurrence, they will be able to provide insight into your spiritual and personal growth when reviewing your journal at later points in time.

May 14, 1994

Today, I graduated from Clark Atlanta University's Graduate School of Social Work with a Master's of Social Work Degree. I'm proud of myself. This is a tremendous accomplishment that I'm glad I'll also be sharing today with many friends and family.

November 1, 1996

An order for 2 copies of *In Search Of Soul* was in my P.O. Box. This is the 1st order for this book in over a year.

February 8, 1997

I read an article in a magazine that Mercury Records is starting a new record label that will produce 20 albums of poetry in the next two and a half years. There is a market for poetry! I just need to be persistent and patient in promoting and marketing my books and myself. For, there is an interested audience.

February 14, 1997

1st 1000 copies of *Mind Games* are in print and I can pick them up today. Finally!!!!!
    Happy Valentine's Day!!!!

May 12, 1999

I can't believe I'm 30 years of age today. Happy Birthday, Anthony!!!!

November 7, 2004

I just finished the final draft of *Healing through Writing*!!!! I have been writing on it for almost seven years. I am so happy I was able to meet my goals and finally give shape to my project. I need to go and celebrate!!!!

RANDOM THOUGHTS/DAILY LIFE QUESTIONS

In recording one's thoughts, one may initiate a process of questioning in an effort to find answers, resolve inner conflicts, and organize ideas. One can make notes about concepts, ideas, or beliefs, which haven't been fully organized and formulated in your mind. One of the most difficult things about recording thoughts and ideas is that it can become very frustrating to try to piece together and organize thoughts in a coherent manner. Successfully synthesizing your thoughts and ideas is generally dependent upon several factors.

First, one should develop the habit of consistently recording new thoughts as they surface. Second, one must learn to exercise patience with the process of fitting the pieces together. This process is similar to putting together all of the pieces to a very complex puzzle or solving an elaborate math problem. All of the pieces must first be laid out and then one can begin to piece by piece put the puzzle together. In recording Random Thoughts and Daily Life Questions one must allow information to flow freely without questioning or trying to make sense of it. This is done with a focus on capturing ideas, intuitions and spiritual insights that are being transmitted while they can be easily accessed by the conscious mind. Once the process of spontaneous writing has been completed, one can organize and interpret what one has written.

Example #1

What is Happiness?
    Having a sense of why you were born.
        Fulfilling one's life purpose.
Being at peace with one's self despite current life circumstances and negative influences in one's environment.
Feeling a connectedness to where one has come from and where one shall return.

Happiness has something to do with:
    Feeling good about who you are as a Person.
    Feeling good about what you are doing with your life.

Example #2

The truth can hurt
especially when
we've been lying to ourselves.

Who wants to see
things as they really are
especially when,
they're not the way
you want them to be.

So many things
are out of our control

that
it doesn't make sense
to cry over spilled milk.

I'm
making everyone's life miserable
trying to meet my own needs.

Some people live their life
through others,
or relive their pain
Again & Again

because they never
let go of the past.

We all have wounds
we must personally tend to.

Everyone's bitter for a reason.
We may not know why?

But, everyone's
bitter for a reason.

Dangling
on a limb

detached
disconnected from
the tree
the root of life.

Nothin' comes easy
but the rain

and sometimes,
it pourssss!!!!!!

Life drips like a faucet.

Before you know it,
it's gone down the drain.

GOALS

Method #1

Goals can serve as a motivational tool as well as to provide a sense of direction in any given area. I have selected to share with you examples of goals that I have recorded in my journal to illustrate the benefit of recording goals to maintain one's commitment to the Growth Process. The goals listed in the following examples are derived from methods taken from two sources. The first example is a method of writing goals that is based upon a Buddhist belief in achieving the right vibrations to materialize one's desires. The phrase "Nam Myoho Renge Kyo" means, "The mystic law of cause and effect." A friend who exercises the Buddhist Faith shared with me how the process works. Twelve goals are listed and one chants, "Nam Myoho Renge Kyo" with one's particular goals in mind to access the vibrations needed to materialize one's desires. While I am not an expert on Buddhism or chanting, I was impressed by the concept of being specific about what you want in life and having the discipline to remain focused on the fulfillment of this desire until it is materialized.

(NAM MYOHO RENGE KYO—1998)

1. Have the freedom to devote more time to my spiritual development

    Make it a way of Life

2. Start earning a living by doing things that I really enjoy doing

    Writing & Creating

3. Become self-employed

4. Schedule first *Healing through Writing* workshop in the next month.

5. Achieve long-term success with *Healing through Writing Workshop* (Help People, Help Myself) Be In Tune With Purpose, Timing, & Cost

6. Surround myself with positive-minded people (don't feel guilty for setting limits and boundaries with people who drain my energy)

7. Work on expanding circle of people who are like-minded and like-spirited

    Call friends who are loving, understanding, and supportive at least once a month and schedule to see them at least once a month

8. Accept full responsibility for shaping my destiny

    Let Go of Past

9. Become more clear about what Happiness is

    How do I define it? What actually is it?

    Incorporate with loving others & myself

10. Live my life focused on Reciprocity—Giving & Receiving, Helping Others

11. Develop a mindset of expectancy

    Power of the mind, My ability to create—shape my reality

12. Become more disciplined in my diet and exercising regularly

Method #2

The second set of examples is taken from a method outlined in Napoleon Hill's book *Think and Grow Rich* in which he discusses the power of autosuggestion. The author suggests that through daily auditory and visual repetition of specific instructions, one can generate the emotional vibrations required to influence the subconscious mind to materialize one's intense desires. The author illustrates how the power of autosuggestion can be utilized by providing an outline for daily repetition. His formula for materializing desires for material wealth includes six steps. Below, I provide examples of how I have for years used this method to visualize and ultimately to materialize financial goals as well as spiritual goals.

Financial Goals

My desire is to earn $1 million a year by age 40, May 12, 2009.

In return for the money, I intend to give spiritual, emotional and practical insight through the creative form of poetry, prose and music.

I believe that I will have this money in my possession. My faith is so strong that I can now see this money before my eyes. I can touch it with my hands. It is now awaiting transfer to me at this time and in the proportion that I deliver the service that I intend to render for it. I am awaiting a plan by which to accumulate this money and I will follow it when it is received.

Spiritual Goals

My desire is to experience health, peace, love, fulfillment, happiness, sexual and creative expression; mental, emotional, spiritual and monetary prosperity every moment of my existence.

In return for this abundant life, I will share my gifts and the fruits of my labor with those who are in need. I will offer spiritual, emotional and monetary support to individuals and groups who are working toward the greater evolution of humanity.

I believe that an abundant life is attainable in this lifetime. I will remain steadfast in maintaining a state of mind that promotes "freedom" of spirit and prosperity. I know that nothing happens by coincidence, and I will remain alert to see my prosperity unfolding.

Method #3

The third set of goals represents a range of personal goals that can be developed by an individual encompassing various aspects of maintaining one's well-being. I refer to these goals as Step-by-Step Goals because the emphasis of the exercise is placed on outlining how one can accomplish his or her goals 'step-by-step" within given timelines. The greatest benefit is that one is able to focus on taking small steps in accomplishing one's long-term goals as opposed to placing too much emphasis on accomplishing one's ultimate goal all at once. In other words, Step-by-Step Goals force one to take small steps and to be patient with the process of focusing on one's growth and development one day at a time.

A second benefit is that, in establishing increments, one is more inclined to set realistic goals because one can more objectively view what is required to achieve one's long-term goals. This includes the flexibility that is provided in developing Step-by-Step Goals as one is able to change the timelines with regards to ensuring that goals are based upon realistic expectations. A final benefit is that one can feel a sense of accomplishment with successfully completing each small goal. Having opportunities to be rewarded more frequently for some is essential in their maintaining their motivation.

The following pages include five Step-by-Step Goal exercises encompassing various aspects of maintaining one's well-being. The first exercise has been completed as an example. Please complete at least one of the other exercises before moving on to the next chapter of this workbook.

RECREATION/EXERCISE GOALS

TODAY

    I will jump rope for 1 minute.

THIS WEEK

    I will jump rope for 1 minute every other day.

THIS MONTH

    Week 2—I will jump rope for 2 minutes every other day.
    Week 3—I will jump rope for 2 minutes and do 50 push ups every other day.
    Week 4—I will jump rope for 3 minutes and do 50 push ups every other day.

3 MONTHS

    I will jump rope for 5 minutes and do 100 push ups every other day.

6 MONTHS

    I will jump rope for 8 minutes and do 150 push ups every other day.

1 YEAR

    I will jump rope for 10 minutes and do 200 pushups every other day.

SPIRITUAL GOALS

TODAY

THIS WEEK

THIS MONTH

3 MONTHS

6 MONTHS

1 YEAR

RELATIONSHIP GOALS

TODAY

THIS WEEK

THIS MONTH

3 MONTHS

6 MONTHS

1 YEAR

FINANCIAL GOALS

TODAY

THIS WEEK

THIS MONTH

3 MONTHS

6 MONTHS

1 YEAR

CAREER GOALS

TODAY

THIS WEEK

THIS MONTH

3 MONTHS

6 MONTHS

1 YEAR

Opening Up

THE POWER OF BELIEFS

Healing through Writing addresses mental as well as emotional obstacles to writing. One must first change the way one thinks about emotions so that one can allow a greater range of expression. Writing, therefore, can be approached with an open mind. This begins with understanding and believing that emotion itself is not negative. It is the avoidance of emotional expression that is negative. For, suppression of emotion in turn limits one's range of freedom in relating to others, one's ability to maintain a healthy internal balance of thought, and one's understanding of self.

For instance, a basketball player who is pumped about a big game is filled with emotion. Yet, how he channels his emotion will dictate the success he has in being self-directed. The same is true about life. If someone makes you angry, your telling that person that you are angry is not necessarily unhealthy. It is how and why you tell that person you're angry that makes a big difference.

Many emotions we feel and experience are more than appropriate considering the situation or given context. Often, what we may fear in acknowledging the fullness and depth of our emotions is that we will be overwhelmed by our emotions and become irrational. We become fearful of not being in control of our behavior or thoughts or of making decisions that we may later regret. Though we may fear the potential harm of fully identifying with the intensity of our emotions, we may fail to fully grasp the potential harm to our mental and physical well-being caused by the continual suppression of our emotions. Statements such as, "I shouldn't feel the way I feel" typify a belief system in which an individual questions the power and beauty of emotional expression. Often, unresolved feelings of guilt and shame fuel this type of belief system. As a result, a part of our emotional selves shuts down.

In addition, a commitment to the growth process requires practice to improve one's ability to express his or her thoughts and emotions through writing and in one's daily interactions with others. Moreover, it entails having an understanding that writing for the purpose of self-expression and self-awareness means writing without being judgmental. There is no need for judgment, because feelings are neither right nor wrong. To be critical is to be concerned with other people's ability to relate to what one is saying and how one chooses to say it. In writing, all that matters is the ability to express one's self in the form that is most adequate or comfortable. That you have said it in a form that is most relative and comfortable for you is what is most significant. In other words, the only thing worth judging is how free one is allowing oneself to be to express what one honestly feels in the moment.

To write with such openness, one must view the pen and paper as one's ally and as a vehicle for self-expression. One must believe that one's relationship between one's emotions and one's journal is necessary and significant. It is because one's skill as a writer is not as significant as one's openness and one's honesty. If one is open, honest, and committed to writing on a daily or consistent basis, in time one will develop the ability to accurately express one's emotions. Additionally, if one has not cleared one's mind of the negative thoughts associated with being aware of and expressing one's emotions, one will not experience the freedom necessary to facilitate one's own Inner Healing and Growth Process. If one has an intense desire to experience greater freedom of emotional expression, evaluating one's belief system is essential for beginning the process of removing emotional barriers. If examining one's belief system is not effective in removing emotional barriers, then it is likely that one is not yet at a place in which one is ready or able to fully digest the intensity and depth of one's underlying emotions. It may take more time to heal one's wounds, but practicing writing about even less intense personal experiences or consistently receiving the external support of a mentor, individual, or group therapist who can convey understanding will eventually pay off. However, before challenging you to closely examine your beliefs, let us briefly discuss beliefs and their significance in our efforts to achieve personal and spiritual goals.

Each of us may have varying definitions of beliefs, but here they are to be understood as, "What one has come to think of as Truth and what one perceives as Reality." The irony is that while we may indeed be very passionate about or protective of our system of beliefs, they don't always represent an objective Truth. Of equal significance is possessing beliefs that contradict and do not support our personal goals. If I say, for instance that I believe that, "My growth is limited" and that "I can't change who I am," my negative thoughts would subsequently be competing with any personal motivation that I may have to change or grow. The same would be true of someone who says that he or she wants to be a millionaire but thinks that money is evil. Thus, one cannot put his heart and soul into one's goal because of one's contradictory beliefs. Consequently, one will not be able to achieve one's goal on one's own efforts, at least not without feeling guilty or unworthy, even if the goal is finally attained.

Jane Roberts, in her book *The Nature of Personal Reality,* addresses the power of our conscious and unconscious beliefs in materializing our personal reality. She contends that the power of our beliefs extends far beyond the parameters of gender and culture. We are like artists who paint a picture of our own personal reality by the beliefs we hold. As Roberts explains, in the long run our beliefs will play themselves out and create an outer material existence of our internal conscious and unconscious patterns of thought and emotion. In light of the above, *Healing through Writing,* attempts to encourage individuals to become more aware of their beliefs as well as of the positive and negative impact that they may have on their lives. Even more, this book urges one to commit oneself to a process of strengthening beliefs that produce positive outcomes and eliminating those that produce negative outcomes.

Beliefs are extremely powerful because they shape our view of reality and dictate the direction of our actions and reactions. Unfortunately, many of us do not realize exactly what we believe. In many instances, we are unwilling to reevaluate our beliefs even in light of additional information that may prove conflicting or contradictory to our personal goals. This may be true because we ultimately know that when our beliefs change, we must change.

PLEASE STOP

Take a moment to reflect on what you believe in your personal life and then complete the exercise on the following page.

PERSONAL BELIEFS

About Myself

About Others

About Life

What beliefs do I have that produce positive outcomes in my life?

What beliefs do I have that produce negative outcomes in my life?

I am sure that if you honestly completed the exercise, you were surprised to discover some of your beliefs. In evaluating them, I hope that you seriously considered the impact that some may have on your freedom and openness to emotional expression as part of your Inner Healing and Growth Process.

If you experienced difficulty completing the exercise or relating your personal beliefs to obstacles in your personal life, review example in Appendix A.

"THE POWER OF BELIEFS"

We,
Sometimes,
Create our own depression—
Not necessarily life circumstances.

Projecting
Our thoughts
and emotions
into material reality.

We,
Sometimes,
Create our own depression—
By how we view the world,
Ourselves
And others

Not accepting
That there is a human,
Natural response
And a grieving process
to every life event.

Not fully realizing
That life
Represents
A mirror image
Of what we
Believe.

We,
Therefore,
Believe things
That we did not know
We believed.

Eventually discovering,
That often,
We believe things
Because....

We don't know
what else
To
believe.

REBUILDING YOUR SYSTEM OF BELIEFS

What we believe is inextricably related to the way we choose to live our lives and the decisions we make. Whether we are fully conscious or not of our beliefs, they directly impact every aspect of our daily lives. Our thoughts and emotions are filtered through our system of beliefs which includes our beliefs about expressing emotion, spiritual growth, relationships, and money among others. Ultimately, it is our beliefs that guide our behavior and shape our assessment of the outcome of various life circumstances. We, for example, entertain many thoughts and are aware of many emotions, but our reactions to what we think and feel is a direct indication of what we believe—our belief system. This, then, results in our altering or maintaining our current belief system and actions.

In her book *In the Meantime: Finding Yourself and the Love You Want*, Iyanla Vanzant uses the analogy of a house to illustrate the various levels we attain in the process of claiming our personal power to shape the direction of our lives. She relates our spiritual growth and development to the challenges that we must confront and overcome as we work our way up from the basement to the attic. *Healing through Writing* borrows from this analogy of a house representing a mirror of ourselves and our personal development. More specifically, *Healing through Writing* is a tool that can be utilized to take personal inventory of one's emotional and spiritual well-being and to repair or rebuild those parts of the house that need mending.

Visually, I have found it useful to encourage clients to conceptualize the analogy of our inner and outer selves representing an emotional house that we are responsible for maintaining. If this emotional house has not been properly built or if one is not used to taking personal inventory of the house, one may not even realize how much has been neglected or even where damage has occurred. Under these circumstances, it is critical that one must take personal inventory. One must assess the damages to his house and determine if one has been living in a house, which only provides physical shelter, or in a home, which provides nurturance and emotional well-being. One must ask oneself, "Has a true sense of peace and contentment been established and maintained in my emotional house?" If the answer is, "No!," then, this means that one must first commit oneself to developing a greater sense of self-awareness of the different dimensions and functions of one's emotional house.

To be sure, one must give oneself permission to begin the work of fully absorbing himself in caring for his emotional needs. This usually begins with tearing down certain values, beliefs, and negative thinking that has resided in his emotional house. In doing so, bad habits, feelings of insecurity, broken and unmended relationships are revealed. It is now only that one can begin the process of rebuilding or reconstructing one's emotional house with beliefs that are in alignment with the best of who one can be as opposed to living out of the definitions or expectations of others. This often includes a process of mending torn relationships and/or embracing new, healthier relationships. Unfortunately, even as adults, many of us experience extreme guilt for isolating ourselves from family and friends to nurture ourselves, to do what is best for us even though it is essential to our well-being. This is particularly difficult when we have to end or terminate certain relationships that no longer serve meaningful or healthy purposes in our lives.

Now that the damages have been assessed, one can begin to repair or rebuild. The irony is that many individuals have been aware of the damages to their emotional house for some time, but for various reasons never moved on to the process of repairing the damage. This may be due to the difficulty of trusting others to help or simply from lacking the knowledge of how to repair the damage. One also may intuitively start the process of tearing down their negative, unproductive system of beliefs but stop because the process may turn out to be too painful and tedious. One feels or fears being overwhelmed with emotion and decides that he or she will learn to live with things the way they are. Nonetheless, like anything in life, time has a way of catching up with us. Whether it's five, ten or twenty years from now, some emotional aspect of oneself that has been neglected may suddenly reappear.

Regardless of the reasons for not moving forward in the process, when one neglects minor damages, they may eventually turn into major damages. What this entails is that large portions or even the entire house may need to be torn down and rebuilt. This is why the initial focus must be to first determine the extent of the damage by honestly asking oneself whether one's current emotional house of values, beliefs and thoughts is working for oneself? In the end, it is often not until some traumatic or life-changing event, such as forming a deeply intimate relationship, becoming a parent, or the death of a loved one that we are compelled to honestly and completely reevaluate our system of beliefs.

PICKING UP THE PEN

Thus far, we have discussed various elements that may comprise a journal and the positive and negative impact that our beliefs may have on our freedom of emotional expression, spiritual and emotional growth. Let us now shift the focus of discussion to the actual process of writing, of putting one's thoughts, emotions, and ideas on paper.

The initial step, as in most instances, can be the most difficult step. When you prepare to write, it is vital that as part of your commitment to the growth process you view writing as a daily ritual or daily exercise. If you are an experienced journal or diary writer, this may not be as significant. But if you are a beginner, it is paramount that writing is considered in light of your expectations to improve your ability as a writer and expand your self-awareness. The six steps listed below may be used for beginners and for experienced writers when experiencing difficulty getting into the flow of writing or opening up emotionally.

Set A Time that is best for you to concentrate and focus your energy (morning, afternoon, after dinner, before bed, and so on) when you can still recall many of the significant events of the day. My mind is most clear early in the morning or late at night. Whenever you decide to set it, make sure you give ample time to unwind and transition from your previous activity. For instance, instead of trying to immediately write, take a few moments to pause and reflect on recent events. This may prove beneficial in providing some initial sense of organization to your thoughts and emotions.

Choose a comfortable location to write. Think of a relaxing environment in which you are not likely to be interrupted or distracted. Also, consider a location in your home or office where you feel the greatest sense of peace or positive energy.

Set the mood. Once you have set a time and located a comfortable, relaxing environment, you will have to determine whether a certain style of music will be required to set the mood. It is important that both your mind and body are calm and relaxed, enabling you to channel your energy on your inner self. For most beginners, music will be necessary to help them sustain their focus. Even after years of practice and experience, there are still times when it is extremely difficult for me to identify or express my intense emotions without the aid of some music that resonates with my mood. The right music for the right mood helps me to relax and become more open to my thoughts and emotions. With practice and time, you will also be able to identify the source of your emotions and express them.

Focus on the music. Sit with your legs folded, close your eyes, and take long, slow, deep breathes to relax your body and clear your mind. As you breathe, inhale through your nose and exhale through your mouth. When inhaling, focus on taking in positive energy and filling your lungs and chest with air. While slowly exhaling, focus on releasing negative energy. Be careful of the pace of your breathing as to not become dizzy. Then ask yourself, "How do I feel?" as you continue taking long, slow deep breaths and gradually become content with silence and stillness. Even if no thoughts come to mind, there is therapeutic value in sitting in silence with your mind and body completely relaxed. Even though you have closed your eyes, begin writing as soon as you become conscious of the thoughts that enter your mind or as you begin to feel emotions surfacing. Be patient with the process, and if you lose your thoughts, simply refocus on the music. Also, remind yourself that this is a process that takes time, especially if there are years of underlying emotion that have not been fully acknowledged or identified.

Write for yourself. Release expectations of others and the urge to judge your emotions. In learning to accept your emotions, you are learning to accept yourself where you are in your process of spiritual growth and self-awareness.

Take small steps. On a daily basis, celebrate each accomplishment. Congratulate yourself for having the discipline to write, even if for only five minutes, a realistic goal for the first week. Focus on consistency and detail. Remember that with time and practice you will develop the ability to honestly and succinctly express your thoughts and emotions through the healthy medium of writing.

Continuing with the six steps to "Picking Up the Pen" listed above, the following pages are designed to challenge you to begin practicing writing on a daily basis. More specifically, you are asked to **commit to writing, for a minimum of five minutes per day, for the next five days.** While you are encouraged to use any of the exercises listed in Appendixes B, C, and D, the emphasis should be placed on your commitment to writing for the next five days, even if it is just your random thoughts. And, then, each day before beginning to write, you can decide whether or not to spontaneously write what you are thinking or feeling or to use any of the exercises provided in the Appendixes as a structured outline to help you organize your thoughts. For, day to day, our emotional and spiritual needs vary, as we are confronted with new challenges.

DAY 1

DAY 2

DAY 3

DAY 4

DAY 5

"THE TRUEST EXPRESSION"

Yes, There is Power
In Emotion
If we
follow them

All the way
Through.

For, our Emotions
Eventually, in time,
Bring us to a Place
Of Clarity
About not just
Why we feel
What we feel

But, what we now
Think is the best
Thing for us
To do!!!!

Fully
Understanding the Reality
And Depth
Of Our Emotions

That despite
How difficult,
How challenging
It is to get to the source

To reach the Depth,
The Core
Of Our Emotions

That,
Inevitably,
We Must Go Through
Our Emotions
Before We Can
Let Go of Our Emotions.

For, this is
The Truest Expression
Of Our Emotions.

Learning to be Honest with Ourselves
In Each and Every Moment.

To Heed the Wisdom
Of Our Internal Voice -
Of Knowing and Understanding
Without Reasons Seen
Or Known.

Learning to act
without further ponderance
Of Why it is
That we feel the way
We feel
Or,
Think the way
We think.

This is
The Truest Expression
Of Our Emotions.

Leading us to
The Source
Of Our Being,

To Greater Wisdom,
To Increased Character & Spiritual Depth.

This Is

The Truest Expression
Of Our Emotions!!!!

PART II
Emotional and Spiritual Growth

Growth and Inner Healing

Part I of *Healing through Writing* focuses on the concept of writing as a tool for personal growth and the actual process of writing on a daily or consistent basis. Part I concluded with the reader being challenged to commit to writing for a minimum of five minutes a day for five consecutive days. If you fulfilled this commitment, you should have gained a sense of the range of thoughts and emotions that we experience on a daily basis. Undoubtedly, you should have gained a glimpse of how our emotional and spiritual growth can be facilitated through the disciplined exercise of writing on a daily or consistent basis and of the focus and concentration that is required to maximize the benefits of writing.

Part II of *Healing through Writing* focuses on describing and outlining the various stages of emotional and spiritual growth and introducing a tool for self-inventory of personal growth. In describing and outlining the various stages, we will first begin with a discussion of the interconnectedness of inner healing and spiritual growth. They represent the process through which we build, rebuild, and maintain our emotional foundation. The outcome of our tireless efforts of time and patience with ourselves and with others is that we may gain freedom of emotional expression and an ability to more consistently maintain balance in our daily lives. While some authors make clear distinctions between inner healing and the growth process, *Healing through Writing* rather views them as being intertwined, directly influencing each other.

Equally, I have found them both to be directly related to expanding self-awareness. As an individual experiences greater freedom and clarity in articulating his or her emotions, one may also find greater spiritual freedom as well. The individual may begin to feel that there are no boundaries or limitations to his or her personal growth and development. At the same time, one may feel a greater sense of personal power to materialize personal goals, dreams, and ideas.

And, just as there are various stages of growth, there also are various stages of healing. Both occur spontaneously, as well as in cycles. For instance, we may periodically face similar events and intrapersonal milestones such as the anniversary of the death of a loved one, unresolved anger towards authority figures, being in love or experiencing greater vulnerability or intimacy. Unfortunately, few of us are conscious of the impact that recurring patterns or cycles have on our daily emotional states of existence. More significantly, few of us understand or are aware of emotional and internal spiritual growth processes as they are occurring in our daily lives. Nonetheless, the flexibility with which we are able to respond most effectively to major life events and intrapersonal milestones is dependent upon the degree of emotional, intellectual, and spiritual awareness we have at given points in time.

When we are unable to gain insight to the source of our own emotional dilemmas we, as a result, are unable to consistently find long-term solutions. And, even when we identify meaningful solutions, many of us lack the courage and discipline to follow through with the identified or recommended remedy for restoring emotional equilibrium. In doing so, we fail to accept responsibility for recurring unhealthy emotional themes and patterns in our lives such as failing to end unhealthy intimate relationships or failing to set boundaries with others. Our personal development stagnates because we continuously arrive at erroneous conclusions and repeat the same patterns of making unhealthy decisions. This is primarily due to our inability to decipher concurrent processes or themes and their parallel relationship to our thoughts and beliefs. For, as cycles and challenges are repeating themselves in our lives, we fail to determine if we are going with the flow of resolving our emotional dilemmas or going against it.

A classic example of limited self-awareness or denial occurs when we instinctively know that we need to take time for ourselves because we are emotionally and mentally worn down. However, we keep trying to keep up with life's increasing demands. Eventually, the daily demands of life take such a toll that we are forced to be still. We become ill or simply have no energy to complete tasks. Our bodies shut down on us. This pattern, for many, is a way of life.

There are many reasons why people are resistant to processing and dealing with emotions as they surface. While many negative behavioral patterns are developed during childhood, they are reinforced throughout life.

Often, intense soul searching is required for a breakthrough to occur. The reality is that we have to make a conscious effort to become aware of and deal with our emotions before we can empower ourselves to change them. The same is true of our emotional dilemmas. For, when we are willing to focus on ourselves and not on what surrounds us, solutions to the problem will reveal themselves to us. Deep breathing, meditation, and inner reflection are generally needed to overcome our sense of powerlessness in this particular area and subsequently to develop the courage to confront our emotional dilemmas and the ability to effectively resolve them.

An analogy I use to illustrate the concept of spiritual and emotional growth includes a continual progression through four stages: Denial (Unconsciousness)—Enlightenment (Self-Awareness)—Personal Responsibility—Transformation. The emphasis of this graph is to illustrate the ongoing interplay between our level of self-awareness and our degree of emotional maturity and spiritual depth.

Stages of Emotional and Spiritual Growth

```
Denial        →   Enlightenment  \
  ↕                    ↕            →Personal Responsibility→Transformation
Unconsciousness → Self-Awareness  /
```

Denial/Unconsciousness

Unconsciousness is the lack of awareness of one's internal, spiritual self and how it influences and is influenced by the environment. This usually occurs in conjunction with denial. Denial is an inability or unwillingness to acknowledge the existence of our spiritual and emotional selves and the truths they constantly reveal to us. In many ways, it is like tunnel vision—only seeing what we want to see. This also may include the suppression of some truth that we believe to exist on an intuitive level—an inner knowing—but fear the emotional repercussions of being fully conscious of this truth, such as feeling a sense of guilt or shame.

Self-Awareness/Enlightenment

Self-Awareness is the ability to independently explore and understand the source of one's thoughts, emotions, and behavior (actions). Enlightenment is revelation, the discovery of truth. Enlightenment may, at times specifically refer to truth revealed about oneself but generally is more inclusive of the truth revealed about our lives. Often, it is knowledge attained through traumatic experiences or mental or emotional breakthroughs. In the graph illustrating the stages of emotional and spiritual growth, Personal Responsibility occurs after Enlightenment and Self-Awareness. To argue that Personal Responsibility occurs before Enlightenment is a valid argument.

However, I am suggesting that many people experience different degrees or levels of enlightenment and self-awareness in numerous ways throughout their lives. Yet, we each have the choice of accepting personal responsibility for utilizing, sharing, and expanding the knowledge we attain. Therefore, one who has not accepted Personal Responsibility has not committed himself or herself to developing a frame of mind to consistently receive enlightenment and act upon it. The individual, therefore, is unable to make a true transformation. He or she is unable to embody as part of their character the knowledge that they have attained.

Personal Responsibility

Personal Responsibility is the receptiveness to and acceptance of knowledge or Enlightenment. It is identified by an individual's consistent commitment to incorporating the knowledge attained in one's personal life. Personal Responsibility is the utilization of knowledge attained for the purpose of enhancing one's personal existence, sharing this knowledge with others, and expanding one's inner self to receive further Enlightenment. It symbolizes inner motivation and the conscious exertion of one's will to search for Truth in any of its Infinite Forms. Personal Responsibility also means that one has begun to visualize or imagine his or her own potentiality and has committed oneself to strive towards that perfection.

Transformation

To be transformed is to be made whole, to be made new. This is with regards to certain aspects of the self, because we can never reach complete perfection in this lifetime. But the change, the conversion from what was to what now exists is so radical that it denotes a clear shift in the development of character in the individual. This can be seen through the perceptions of others as well as through self-examination. Most importantly, Transformation is not haphazard. Though we may experience revelation or breakthroughs in growth (Enlightenment), Transformation is the result of our conscious commitment to the Growth Process. When we exercise discipline and have the courage to continue searching for the Truth about unresolved inner conflicts and particular questions raised in The Now of Life, Transformation is inevitable. Thus, it is not only the answer to the question. It is manifested in the quality and character of the person as a result of one's search for and discovery of certain Truths. Ultimately, Transformation personifies the continuous cycle of growth as now having its' own momentum in one's life.

"Transformation"

I stopped trying
To find
Love Outside
Of myself
The Day
I Found Love
Within.

I stopped trying
To Find Faith
In you
When I finally
Found
Faith
Within Myself.

In that Moment
Of Silence
And Quiet Reflection
I found
This Great Revelation.

Then,
It became a part
Of who I am.

Seven Determinants of Emotional and Spiritual Growth

Transformation should be the ultimate goal of our commitment to the Inner Healing/Growth Process. Yet, Transformation should be viewed as various steps to be taken and multiple levels to be attained as opposed to a fixed state of existence. At the same time, our efforts to achieve wholeness and balance should not serve as an indication that we have reached a final destination in our process of maturation. Wholeness simply means that we have developed various aspects of our personality—our ability to think, feel, and have faith, whether we are a man or a woman, such that there is a unique quality about our individuality that is not limited by gender, race, and so on. It means that we have tapped into not only our spiritual essence but also our humanity in that we can move beyond any perceived boundaries in loving and relating to others. Balance represents the work and energy that we must constantly put forth to achieve and maintain a sense of openness and connectedness to the universe and to others.

Our emotional and spiritual growth, therefore, is multi-dimensional and multi-faceted. It has many layers and is simultaneously simplistic and complex. While it is our desire and commitment to transformation that fuels our growth, there are numerous factors that interplay with our internal processes of inner healing and emotional and spiritual growth. I refer to these various factors as **seven determinants of emotional and spiritual growth.** The seven determinants of emotional and spiritual growth listed below relate specifically to the focus of this workbook, which is on empowering individuals to facilitate their own growth and inner healing. In stages of your life when you are "stuck" in your personal growth and seeking ways to motivate yourself or to find answers to difficult life questions, the seven determinants of emotional and spiritual growth are intended to serve as a tool for self-inventory.

Determinant #1

An individual's ability to adopt the belief that we are not only physical beings, but that we are emotional and spiritual beings as well.

It is my belief that an individual who wants to expand beyond personal barriers to one's emotional growth must first adopt the belief that we are not only physical beings, but that we are emotional and spiritual ones as well. This means that one does not place greater emphasis on thinking than on feeling, but understands that both represent elements of truth about life and us in general. In other words, they both reflect aspects of who one is and where one is in his or her personal development. And, in maintaining a high level of simultaneous awareness of one's emotions and thoughts, one is less limited in his or her responses to others and various life situations.

Determinant #2

An individual's ability to develop a sense of clarity about what are some of the healthy and unhealthy forms of self-expression within one's daily life.

Most of us know what upsets us, what triggers us. However, few individuals have identified the most effective strategies and techniques for dealing with their intense emotions. Or, they may simply lack the discipline and will power to utilize these effective strategies and techniques when faced with conflict. An anger management plan or written checklist of anger management techniques (see appendix C) is very beneficial when one is confronted with conflicts. It provides an individual, in advance, with a range of healthy responses to various situations that trigger intense emotion. It is because, when our emotions are triggered, we may have a habit of disregarding the impact that our words or actions will physically or emotionally have on others.

Though we each have different ways of expressing and dealing with our emotions, there is a range of emotion and expression that would generally be considered healthy or unhealthy in a given context or situation. For example, an introverted person who has no outward reaction to the death of a loved one could be perceived as void of emotion. Likewise, an extroverted person destroying property and harming others to vent his or her frustration would be perceived as violent and out of control. Thus, the suppression of our emotions and the over zealousness in expressing our emotions can both represent unhealthy forms of self-expression. Ultimately, the expression of our emotions must always be evaluated in the context of the precipitating event.

Determinant #3

An individual's ability to clearly define healthy love in interpersonal relationships and to incorporate it into one's daily life.

This degree of emotional and spiritual maturity is clearly observed in an individual's ability to accept full responsibility for the manifestation of recurring patterns of unhealthy relationships and unhealthy emotional dilemmas. An individual, for example, may continue to draw into one's life intimate partners who have unhealthy habits of dealing with their emotions and unhealthy concepts of love. This may range from substance abuse or other addictions to fear of intimacy and the inability to express love. The individual, as a result, has a habit of forming unhealthy committal relationships. To break this unhealthy pattern, the individual first must become aware of any limitations within themselves to meet their own emotional needs. In doing so, one is able to develop a barometer for assessing what needs from a partner are healthy and which ones are unhealthy. This barometer will also support the development of some form of conscience that serves, not simply to induce guilt, but to also remind the individual of previously self-determined boundaries for ensuring healthy interaction with others. For one, one must know when to take time for oneself, but this entails a high degree of self-awareness. This is critical, given the expectations that other individuals may have of us in their efforts to have their emotional needs met. Therefore, one must not feel guilty for doing what is necessary to maintain a sense of internal and external balance in one's life, including not sacrificing oneself for the other person.

Determinant #4

An individual's ability to make a clear distinction between suffering and struggling.

What does it mean to suffer? For me, to suffer means that I am going through intense pain and anguish not just because of the current challenge or difficulty that I am experiencing but because there is no apparent way to change or remove myself from my current life dilemma or to change how I am feeling. Consequently, there is a sense of helplessness and hopelessness because I am unable to see or believe that I have the ability to secure the necessary external or internal resources or personal power and energy to change my life circumstances. For, in my own life, I have eventually been able to move forward only when I was reminded and was finally willing to accept the reality that my life circumstances would not change overnight. Equally, I had to move to a place of committing myself to, methodically, step-by-step, doing whatever was necessary and within my power to change my life circumstances regardless of the sacrifice. This renewed hope and belief that time and patience with the process of healing will ultimately result in happiness and fulfillment is what many individuals would sometimes refer to as "faith" in God. I, however, am referring not just to the faith in God but also to the faith we have in ourselves and in our God-given ability and right to be happy and to be at peace with ourselves. For, if one does not believe that he or she has a right to be happy, one, then, will never fully identify with and own the internal and external resources that God makes available for the dramatic change to occur in our lives.

This leads us to what it means to struggle. To struggle means that there is forward progress because the individual has some sense of hope though he or she may be enduring a very difficult and painful process. Though one may have faith in God and in oneself and is fully committed and willing to do whatever it takes to accept responsibility for experiencing happiness and fulfillment, it still may take a lot of time and energy to finally experience the peace, happiness, and fulfillment that one has longed for. However, because one may have a sense of faith or hope in his or her internal and external resources and possibly a clear plan or goal, which one is trying to attain, one has something to motivate oneself to keep moving forward with a positive or optimistic attitude. One may even understand

and accept that the road may continue to be very difficult, but is willing to remain committed to the process of reconstructing one's life.

Emotional suffering, on the other hand, causes one to lose energy, faith, and sometimes even a sense of purpose for living. Without a sense of purpose and without hope, an individual will not feel that suffering has its purpose and that one must learn from it. This is why it is so critical for an individual to be able to make a clear distinction between suffering and struggling, so that when experiencing adversity in one's life, one will have the ability to look beyond his or her circumstances and to focus on what is within one's power to change one's life circumstances. One must be able to understand and accept that in every situation one has the ability to choose to focus either on the negative or on the positive. Regardless of how difficult the challenge, for there to be forward progress, one must exercise some measure of faith. In other words, one has the choice to see the glass as half empty or as half full.

Please be aware as to not misinterpret this statement. For, I am not disregarding experiences in which there are blatant acts of violence, oppression, or some form of physical or mental illness, and so on. Rather, I am referring to life situations within the context of adults who do possess the ability to exercise a certain degree of independence in their lives. My argument, then, is that in most situations we do have the ability to change our surroundings, our friends, and ultimately our perspective on our life circumstances. Yet, we, too often because of our emotional and mental state, fail to focus on what aspects of our lives we really do have control over. Instead, we frequently choose to only focus on the things we do not have control of and use this as an excuse for our deciding to settle for less or as a reason to blame our circumstances on someone or something else. We, consequently, will only continue to feel bitter, frustrated, victimized, and unable to make forward progress with this frame of mind. We will not be able to take the initial steps towards improving our life circumstances because self-doubt and the obstacles we may have to overcome, in our minds, remain greater than the circumstances themselves.

For instance, if we are unhappy with our job, we can choose to change jobs. We can decide to make a sacrifice and return to school, move to another state or accept another job possibly for less pay until we are presented with a better opportunity. However, if we do not have a strong conviction and a high level of determination to pursue and attain a more fulfilling occupation, we will not have the courage to take the initial steps that will open the door to a new job or new career possibilities.

Amazingly, for some individuals, making such decisions and taking risks are as simple as breathing. For others, taking the initial steps and sticking with their plan frequently becomes very complicated because of the sense of obligation they feel to their children, spouse, or possibly other family members. Feelings of fear and anxiety may also be compounded by financial concerns. In the end, regardless of the sacrifices such people may have to make and the obstacles that may have to be overcome, one ultimately does have free will to choose and create the level of contentment one will have in one's life.

Determinant #5

An individual's ability to understand and accept that inner healing and growth are long-term processes.

The stages of emotional and spiritual development are ongoing and unlimited. And, while an individual may experience periods of rapid growth and maturity at given stages and transitions of his or her life, change, generally, does not happen overnight. It is a slow and gradual process that requires the commitment of time, energy, and patience. Unfortunately, for many, the concept of "process" is one of the most frightening aspects of healing and personal growth. I often have found this to be true through my observations as a therapist, as a workshop facilitator, and in my relations with significant others. It is as though on an intuitive level, when an individual has developed a habit of suppressing his or her emotions, one knows that there exists a potential floodgate of emotions that will pour out if one allows a drip to drain from the faucet. Suppression, then, becomes a necessity for coping with the intensity of one's emotions and in many instances avoiding or limiting one's vulnerability to others. Yet, the reality is that if there were no fear of a flood, there would be no need for a damn. In other words, if emotion is not given the opportunity to build up or become excessive, in the long-term it can not be harmful, negative, or damaging to ourselves or to others.

I have also discovered that coming to terms with this aspect of personal growth can be especially difficult for individuals who are seeking immediate answers to their emotional dilemma or crisis. Therefore, to suggest that what an individual is presently feeling may continue to be a part of one's inner existence for an extended period of time can seem overwhelming because some associate it with more suffering. This makes it even more difficult to see the light at the end of the tunnel—to see beyond the pain. And without feeling loved and not having a consistently available support system, it is easy to understand why such feeling and attitude would prevail.

Sometimes, however, the answer to our dilemmas and emotional relief will present itself only when we are willing to put our ego aside and ask for help. Only when we can move beyond our shame in expressing our deepest vulnerabilities are we finally able to open ourselves to receiving the emotional and physical support that is needed not only to sustain our existence, but also to move us to a place of balance and wholeness. To me, this is symbolic of the saying, "When the student is ready, the teacher will appear." In other words, we just have to be open, patient with the process, and work hard to maintain an attitude of expectancy.

Determinant #6

An individual's ability to focus more energy on materializing his or her desires and beliefs, instead of on perceived obstacles.

Long-term success in the materialization and fulfillment of one's dreams, goals and desires is achieved through years of practicing how to focus one's mental and emotional energy on expected outcomes. This requires a conscious choice and effort to create an attitude and mindset of expectancy. For most, this is accomplished through daily rituals and exercises of meditation, visualization, and goal setting. Thus, there is constant reinforcement of one's conscious and subconscious desires. The individual is consistently identifying areas within one's emotional make-up that are obstacles to one's ability to focus on the positive as opposed to the negative to ensure that one's thoughts and beliefs support and are in alignment with one's desires and goals. The individual also recognizes that one's ability to maintain a positive focus is supported or hindered by his or her circle of family and friends. Therefore, one must be willing to make the necessary adjustments within these circles to ensure that he or she is able to maintain a positive, healthy mindset.

Determinant #7

An individual's ability to achieve some level of discipline when it comes to incorporating writing and other rituals in one's daily life.

As discussed in Determinant #6, daily rituals and visualization are required to constantly reinforce positive thinking and to maintain emotional balance. However, every individual is different. Some need more positive reinforcement than others. Some individuals are able to maintain a high level of self-awareness and emotional balance without needing to adhere to a strict diet of daily mental and emotional exercises and rituals. Nevertheless, we all require some degree of participation in certain activities and outlets to maintain emotional equilibrium. This is why I strongly recommend developing a mental or written stress management plan (see appendix D) that includes any range of extra curricular activities, a food diet and a routine of physical exercise. This plan is fine-tuned by experimenting with different activities in response to different stressors.

Regardless of what is needed to maintain balance, our understanding of ourselves and utilizing this understanding of self is what allows us to remain centered.

Shaping Our Daily Reality

The time has now come for you to make a choice to use the information presented in this workbook to make forward progress in your spiritual and emotional growth. The purpose of this workbook is to encourage you to find solutions to your emotional dilemmas and to facilitate growth and inner healing through self-empowerment. Self-empowerment is your ability to tap into your internal and external resources to heal yourself and to expand your self-awareness. Whether you are rebuilding your emotional house or simply exploring additional methods and techniques to maintain emotional balance in your life, *Healing through Writing* is a tool that any individual can use in the process of facilitating personal growth. But, for *Healing through Writing* to be of maximum benefit, you must make a personal commitment to spiritual and emotional growth and exercise discipline by taking the time to write on a daily or consistent basis. It is equally important that you set personal goals for writing and for spiritual development that are realistic. You then must have the courage to explore your emotions on a daily basis. This is what fuels your growth, your desire for change. If you possess the ingredients of discipline, desire, and courage, not only will your perceptions about life change, but also those about yourself will change.

We will close with the diagram on the following page illustrating how our daily reality is shaped by many internal and external factors. Nonetheless, the more we are aware of these factors and understand how they negatively and positively influence us, the more we are able to claim and exercise our god-given personal power to shape the direction of our lives.

SHAPING OUR DAILY REALITY

Words
↕
Emotions ↔ Our Daily ↔ Beliefs
Reality
↕
Thoughts

APPENDIX A

PERSONAL BELIEFS

<u>About Myself</u>
My Growth Is Limited.
I Can't Change Who I Am/I Am Who I Am.
I believe that I was put on this earth to fulfill a purpose but I'm not sure what the purpose is.
I'm a survivor.

<u>About Others</u>
There are some good people in the world but most people can't be trusted.
No One Can Understand Me.

<u>About Life</u>
Life Isn't Fair.
Life Is A Struggle.
You're Born And You Die.
Only Rich People Enjoy Life.

<u>What beliefs do I have that produce positive outcomes in my life?</u>
I believe that I was put on this earth to fulfill a purpose but I'm not sure what the purpose is.

<u>What beliefs do I have that produce negative outcomes in my life?</u>
My growth is limited.
I can't change who I am.
No one can understand me.
Life Isn't Fair.
Life Is A Struggle.
You're Born And You Die.
Only Rich People Enjoy Life.

My Beliefs About....

Emotional Expression

Relationships

Love

Money

Appendix B

WHAT IS MY DEFINITION OF LOVE?

WHO HAS LOVED ME?

WHAT WERE THEIR QUALITIES?

LIST THE THINGS THEY DID THAT YOU ASSOCIATE WITH LOVE?

DO I LOVE MYSELF?
    Why? Or Why not?

HOW DO I DEFINE HAPPINESS?

AM I HAPPY?

If the answer is "Yes," list 3 reasons why you believe that you are happy.

I am happy because....

If the answer is "No," list 3 things that you believe will make you happy.

I will be happy when....

LIST 3 POSITIVE STATEMENTS TO AFFIRM A POSITIVE MINDSET AND TO MAINTAIN A SENSE OF HAPPINESS IN YOUR LIFE.

To maintain my sense of happiness, I will....

To create a sense of happiness in my life, I will....

LIST 3 POSITIVE STATEMENTS THAT AFFIRM A MINDSET OF SUCCESS.

I am successful because....

APPENDIX C

Anger Management Plan

1. What three things make me most angry?

2. What is unhealthy about the way I deal with each of the three things that make me most angry?

3. What is the first sign that I am getting angry?

4. What is a healthy response to each of the three things that make me most angry?

APPENDIX D

Stress Management Plan

When I am sad or angry
    I will….

When I am emotionally or physically exhausted
    I will….

Extracurricular Activities
    I will….

Food Diet
    I will….

Routine of Physical Exercise
    I will….

NOTES

NOTES

NOTES

References

Akbar, Na'im. *The Community of Self.* Mind Productions, 1985.

Bentz, Valerie Malhotra. *Becoming Mature: Childhood Ghosts and Spirits in Adult Life.* New York: Aldine de Gruyter, 1989.

Bly, Robert. *Iron John.* Vintage, 1992.

Dyer, William. *You'll See It When You Believe It.* William Morrow, 1989.

Hill, Napoleon. *Think & Grow Rich.* Fawcett Crest, 1960.

Kipnis, Aaron R. *Knights Without Armor: A Practical Guide for Men in Quest of Masculine Soul.* Perigee, 1991.

Kiyosaki, Richard. *Rich Dad, Poor Dad.* Warner, 2000.

Liddell, Ellis. *Weatlh Management: Merging Faith with Finance.* ELE Wealth Management, 2004.

Pennebaker, James. *Opening Up: The Healing Power of Expressing Emotions.* The Guilford Press, 1990.

Roberts, Jane. *The Nature of Personal Reality.* Amber-Allen, 1979.

Redfield, James. *The Celestine Prophecy.* Warner, 1993.

Schierse-Leonard, Linda. *The Wounded Woman: Healing the Father-Daughter Relationship.* Shambhala, 1985.

Vanzant, Iyanla. *Acts of Faith: Daily Meditations for People of Color.* New York: Simon & Schuster, 1993.

Vanzant, Iyanla. *In the Meantime: Finding Yourself and the Love You Want.* New York: Simon & Schuster, 1998.

Wilson-Schaef, Anne. *Women's Reality*. Shambhala, 1993.

Zweig, Connie and Jeremiah Abrams. *Meeting The Shadow: The Hidden Power of the Dark Side of Human Nature*. Perigee, 1991.

EMPOWERMENT WORKSHOPS

Anthony D. Parnell, M.S.W. author of *The 7 Laws of Stress Management, Healing through Writing: A Journaling Guide to Emotional & Spiritual Growth, Mind Games* and *In Search of Soul* has developed a series of unique workshops designed to empower individuals to achieve and maintain balance and well-being in one's personal and professional life.

Please register me for one or more of the following workshops (place an "X" next to the workshops of your choice):

_____ "Stress Management" Workshop

- **Learn 7 simple steps for developing a stress management plan**
- **Identify 7 key principles for maintaining balance in your daily life**
- **Increase productivity in your professional and personal life**

(Ideal for 1-Hour Lunch Presentations for business and organizations)

~

_____ "Healing through Writing" Workshop

- **Learn about the spiritual and emotional benefits of keeping a daily journal**
- **Improve your ability to express your thoughts and emotions through writing**
- **Identify ways to more effectively manage stress**

~

_____ "Spiritual Empowerment" Workshop

- Increase awareness of self and barriers to spiritual growth
- Identify tools for self-empowerment to achieve personal goals
- Strengthen spiritual foundation through self-exploration

____ # of Persons Attending (3-Hour Presentation)

____ x $49/person = _____

____ "1-Hour Lunch Presentation" for non-profit organizations and businesses ($199/$299)

____ # of persons attending

___ Mr. ___ Mrs. ___ Ms.

Contact Name_____

Title/Organization_____

Address_____

Office #_____ **Cell #** _____

Please list, in order of preference, dates that you would like to attend a workshop. All workshops, excluding the "1-Hour Lunch Presentations," are scheduled on Saturdays:

_____ _____ _____

To complete registration for a workshop, mail this form along with a cashiers check or money order payable to:

www.NewThoughtManagement.com
2202 South Figueroa Street, #232
Los Angeles, CA 90007
(818) 973-3159
(213) 749-2013

*Registration fee is non-refundable if cancellation is requested less than 48 hours of scheduled workshop.

978-0-595-34642-4
0-595-34642-1

CPSIA information can be obtained
at www.ICGtesting.com
Printed in the USA
LVHW092154160621
690457LV00014B/129